— How to Survive —
HIGH SCHOOL

A NAVIGATION GUIDE AND JOURNAL FOR THE TEEN GIRL

KIMBERLY WILSON DANIEL, M.Ed. GCDF

FOREWARD BY MELANIE SPARKS MYERS

Printed in the United States of America

ISBN-13: 978-1548179908

ISBN-10: 1548179906

Keystone
Instructional Services, Inc.

www.keystoneinstructionalservices.com

CONTENTS

Kimberly Wilson Daniel

Dear Beautiful:

High School is going to be okay. I know it sounds cliché but believe me, your circumstances, whether good or bad, don't make you. They only create a base for who you're going to be. It's up to you to make the negative a positive and the positive a standard.

I want to share with you with a few things I was told at your age that have truly shaped my life:

- No one can ever take away your knowledge. Keep learning!
- It's always okay to ask for help. You don't have to carry the world on your shoulders.
- If you are privileged enough to be able to speak up for the voiceless, never doubt it. Speak up!
- You're not a victim or statistic. You're a survivor. Whatever the battle may be.
- Love yourself first. You're going to be okay. I believe in you.

Sincerely,

"Y", 25, Event Coordinator

<u>Dedication</u>

This book is dedicated to every girl who is about to enter high school. You are beautiful and gifted. You are a precious gift to this world. I know this and it's important for you to know as well. The next four years of your life will bring many new experiences. Through proper guidance, you will develop into a successful young woman who is ready to go out into the world and ignite positive change. You have a voice. You have a purpose. You have what this world needs. Yes, you!

For you to be all you are destined to be, you must choose your path very carefully. Knowing who you want to become and what steps you need to take for that to happen is key. It won't be easy. It will take discipline and perseverance. Not everyone will agree with your convictions so, at times, you will need to be brave enough to stand alone. The friends who start this journey with you may not be by your side at the end so, at times, you will need to be brave enough to walk alone. Not everyone will understand your determination and drive and that's ok because making it to your destination depends on you, not them.

I didn't know all of this when I was your age. I was basically flying by the seat of my pants. I thought I needed everyone to like me. I thought all the cool girls had a boyfriend. I thought it was more important to be social and have fun than to focus and study. No one taught me how to "play the tape to the end" when making choices. Therefore, I thought everything would just work out like I wanted. I guess you can say I was living by the YOLO motto. I didn't know there were specific steps and actions that I should have been taking to ensure things would turn out the way I wanted. Lacking exposure to the right tools and strategies while I was in high school was a contributing factor to my becoming a teen parent. My senior year of high school should have been all about college choice but instead, it was all about taking care of my beautiful baby girl, Meagen. I had goals but no plans and as a result, my goals simply became wishes. Today, not only do I have a goal and a plan, but I also have a MISSION. I created the 3 Cord Strand mission which focuses on inspiring young girls and women to become **Educated**, **Equipped**, and **Empowered**. This book was written to help teen girls accomplish this by exposing them to tools and strategies that will guide them through their high school years and assist them in establishing a solid foundation to build upon once they transition out into the real world.

This book is dedicated to **YOU**. The gifted, smart, and talented young girl who is starting this new journey to becoming a gifted, smart, and talented young woman.

◄──────────────────────────────►

Marie, 24, High School Math Teacher

Life can be a tall glass of lemonade despite the lemons you acquired at birth or throughout life. In other words, life and everything about it is what you make it. Never use the home you came from, your gender, your race, or the people in your life as an excuse not to make your lemonade or make something of yourself. It's all about the mindset you have with life's trials and tribulations: life's lemons.

As a young girl, my life wasn't always full of joy and love. I had a mother who I felt did not want or love me at times. There were times that my two sisters and I lived with our grandmother because my mother simply did not want to be a parent at the time. That damaged me emotionally. I stayed in a neighborhood full of crime, and at any moment, I could have lost my life from being in the wrong place at the wrong time. I kept quiet and bottled up a lot of things. There were many things I saw and experienced as a child that were not okay. Instead of allowing it to make me bitter, I allowed it to make me better.

I knew that education was my way to a better life for myself and my future family. You must take high school very serious. It is a vital step leading to adulthood. Yes, there will be times that you want to give up, but with the help of loving family, caring teachers, and a gracious God, you can push through. You must find people who will keep you focused and level headed. Having people that love you and will listen to you when no one else will is very important. Keeping your problems bottled up can really affect you, and as young ladies, you must learn how to pay

7

less attention to the things you can't change. Put your energy into things that matter. This includes staying away from boys that are no good.

Most teenage boys want one thing and one thing only. Don't allow the opinions of some cute and charming boy define you. You are more than your physical appearance. You have a brain that holds intelligence capable of changing the world. You have a heart capable of loving a husband or children of your own like no other. Get involved in activities that will keep you away from things that are not good for you whether that is a sport, a church, or a job.

If there was one thing I could have changed as a young lady in high school, I would have utilized my lemons more efficiently. I would have learned at an early age how to stop worrying about things that I could not change. I would have taken those lemons and made lemonade. If you don't make your own lemonade, you'll waste your lemons. Lemons teach us lessons. Lemons mold us into greater women each day. Lemons make your lemonade the best lemonade on the block.

←—————————————————→

Foreword

HIGH SCHOOL. Wow. Those two words stir up a lot of feelings inside me. Some of those feelings are bad, but honestly, most of them are extremely good. High school was an amazing experience for me. I have often said that the years I spent in high school were some of the most transformational, most wonderful years of my life. However, I know that my happy memories of high school are no accident. There are very specific reasons why I can think back on those memories with a huge smile on my face. What are those reasons, you ask? The answer to that question is simple—constant support from influential adults in my life, close friends with similar beliefs and goals, clear guidelines of what I did and did not want for my present and future self, and most importantly, my faith in God's provision for my life.

There will be opportunities for rising above and for falling behind...choose wisely. As author Thomas Paine said, "Character is much easier kept than recovered." Simply put, once you tarnish your reputation you can bounce back, but it will be very difficult and it will take a lot of hard work on your part. On the other hand, if you maintain your good reputation by refusing to stray away from your goals and convictions, high school and life, in general, will be much less of a struggle.

In this guide, written by my amazing friend Kim Daniel, you will find wisdom that explains how to build a successful high school career for yourself. Kim touches on many of the crucial components that were so instrumental in my own high school happiness. As Kim explains, you only have one shot at high school. There is no do-over. I promise that you will want to be able to look back five years, fifteen years, and even forty years after high school and smile when recalling your freshmen through senior years. This guide can help you do that.

Don't take this guide lightly. Read it and reread it. Highlight words and sentences that jump out at you. Underline its basic principles and memorize them. Carry this guide with you to school and school related activities. Let Ms. Daniel's words become your mantra for not only surviving high school but thriving in high school. Adopt this guide as your tool to assist you in not just finishing high school, but finishing WELL! You will be forever grateful, I can assure you.

Melanie Sparks Myers, 8th grade ELA teacher

←——————————————————————→

Nijja Vargas, 22, Future Physician's Assistant

I'm not going to pretend to be an expert in high school life but I'd like to share with you what I learned throughout high school and my experiences. My parents were both very supportive of me all throughout high school and pretty strict. I never really went anywhere and they were constantly checking up on my grades. Now that I have graduated college, I look back and appreciate how much they looked out for me. At the time, it may have seemed like a big deal to not go to that party or to not date that guy but now I know that my parents helped keep me focused and safe. Speaking of, "dating that boy"... I just want to share with you a profound knowledge that I sincerely hope you take to heart. You are valuable. You are worth being pursued and you are worth so much. Not every boy is worth your time and if he doesn't treat you with kindness and respect then he is not the one for you. You deserve a guy that respects your decisions and is future focused. You are young, beautiful, and intelligent so don't lose your head over a guy that is not worth your time. I urge you to not be easily swayed by smooth words and no action. Have patience because you deserve prince charming and he will come and pursue you all in God's time.

I did not have any form of social media until I was in college. I used to be upset that my parents wouldn't allow me to do what everyone else was doing and I often felt so out of the loop. However, before I even had social media it brought me drama. People often get very bold when sitting behind a computer screen and Cyberbullying is very real. It is never okay to send harsh messages through the internet. Social media can be a wonderful way to connect with people but take caution. What you post is out there forever for the entire world to see.

No matter how "lame" you may think it is, it is important for you to form relationships with your teachers. Obviously, you are not going to be best friends with every single teacher. However, I promise you there are several to whom you can connect. I had some teachers greatly impact my life. They gave me extra help when needed, life advice when warranted, and helped me get into college by writing my letters of recommendation. Throughout my life, I have always enjoyed school and there are teachers that I miss dearly to this day.

At school, you are ultimately there to learn. That can sometimes be hard to remember because of all the drama, friends, boys, clubs, and sports. Education is something that no one can ever take away from you and your education can take you far in life. You get out of it what you put into it. If you work hard then you can and will succeed. Don't blow it off. To chase your dreams, you must build a solid foundation. It is worth the time and effort and you will be rewarded for it.

I played varsity basketball during my high school days and I was also involved in a couple of honors clubs as well as the Christian club my high school offered. These activities helped to make me a well-rounded individual. That is one of the key characteristics that colleges are searching for in an applicant. It also taught me a lot about life. Although I loved basketball, I learned that there is more to life and that an education is more important. I know that may be hard for some of you to hear but your education is more important than your sport. Your education will take you further in life. Now don't get me wrong, enjoy your sport. Enjoy it completely and fully and if your dream is to play in college then pursue it but know that your sport is not all that you are. You have so much more to offer.

Lastly, if I could go back and change how I did things I would. I wouldn't be so afraid to be myself. I wouldn't be so worried about fitting in or impressing guys. I wouldn't let basketball control my happiness. I would have skipped taking AP classes in favor of dual enrolling in the local college. If you take anything away from this letter I hope it is this - just be yourself, have fun, and work hard. You will be amazed at what you can accomplish. Don't be afraid to ask for help when you need it! It will be worth it in the end. I hope this letter helps you and maybe even inspires you. You can do this.

Introduction

HIGH SCHOOL! YES! I MADE IT!

Now what? What are these next four years really going to be like? I wonder if they *really* put freshmen in the trash can or if they *even* notice the freshmen? What's all this talk about GPA and credits? Oh my, look at these cute boys! These are many of the questions and thoughts that run through the minds of most teen girls as they prepare to embark on this next stage of life. Where are the answers and how can you proceed through high school with rewarding experiences and very few regrets?

High school is a time to explore new possibilities and figure out who you really are. It's like going on a quest. This can be one of the most exciting and rewarding experiences of your life, or it can be a series of wrong decisions that set the scene for one dramatic issue after the other. During this time of exploration, you will begin to discover important characteristics about yourself and others. Some will be good and some not so good; however, the key is to learn as much as possible from the experiences.

This navigation guide provides best practices and relevant advice from a teacher's perspective and from the perspective of young ladies who not too long ago were in your shoes. They all survived high school and have collaborated with me to provide you with strategies for making this the best four years possible. Take heed to their words of wisdom and implement their advice. Don't be in a rush to get through high school. Embrace the journey, the lessons, the ups and the downs, and know that they are all shaping you into the person you are destined to be. Always find time to read and journal your thoughts, questions, and experiences. Seek to find out who you really are in these next few years.

Setting aside a specific time each day to journal is a way for you to unplug from the rest of the world and focus on you and your thoughts. It's a time sit back, relax, and record the events that took place throughout the day and how those events made you feel. You will begin to see this as an effective way of addressing your emotions and behaviors. Over time, you will pinpoint patterns of behavior and address those behaviors and how they contribute to the good or adverse consequences that you experience. This is also a way to plan for your future. Writing out your dreams and aspirations helps you to focus on where you are headed in life. Having clear goals and visions is key to being successful in school. There are journal pages at the end of this navigation guide. Use them to keep record of your daily experiences. Along the journey, go back and reflect on your thoughts and actions so you can monitor your growth.

To blossom into the beautiful woman you are destined to be, you must navigate through the next few years strategically. You must plan these years out and enter high school with a specific plan of action. This requires setting goals and boundaries. I can tell you from my own experiences as well as what I have witnessed as a teacher, goal setting is extremely important. Along with the goals you set, you must also develop a plan of action because without a plan your goal is simply a wish.

When I was young, pretty much every little girl's goal was to be "a baby doctor." I loved babies and I thought it would be cool to be a doctor. I had the goal but there was a key component missing from my goal setting process that prevented me from becoming a pediatrician - the path to accomplishing that goal. The path is the road map you develop that clearly defines how you get from where you are today to where you want to be in the future. It's like beginning with the end in mind. You know where you want to end up, but how do you get there? I'm not just speaking education-wise. Everyone knows to become a pediatrician, you need good grades in high school and undergraduate school so that you can enter a good medical school. That's common knowledge. Most people establish that portion of the goal but forget to set the do's and don'ts for issues that could disrupt the process of obtaining their goal. Things such as friendships, time management, relationships, character, and discipline. What are your standards and boundaries when it comes to those factors? Effective planning in these areas is the hard part. These are the areas where most teen girls experience the most failure. They fail to see them as stumbling blocks until *after* they have stumbled. That was me. I didn't map out my PLAN... so I got sidetracked. If I would have had my plan drawn out and my boundaries and standards set, I would more than likely be writing to you from the viewpoint of Dr. Kimberly W. Daniel. You see, my plan wouldn't have allowed me to stray off course and end up pregnant in high school. My plan wouldn't have allowed me to get off course and get married at the age of 19. My plan would have kept me focused on the end result which was accomplishing my goal of becoming a pediatrician. My path to success was not developed and therefore I was not prepared with strategies to address those situations when they surfaced along my journey. Had the plan been in place, I would have been prepared to avoid anything that was not in line with it. This navigation guide will assist you in developing your plan. Your plan will help you navigate through high school victoriously by moving successfully past the stumbling blocks and distractions that will surface throughout your journey.

←——————————————————————→

Audrina Claxton, 24, Entrepreneur

Growing up, my father wasn't around, but the advice and guidance I received from my mother was essential. I am, and will always be a late bloomer. I also got saved two months after freshman year began. So, to say that I didn't do much "experimenting" was an understatement. When I had trouble being myself, it was my mother who instilled in me the strength to carry on. I didn't really wear jewelry, no makeup whatsoever, and I was a true introvert. When I would look at all the girls who were social butterflies, those girls who had no problem speaking to groups of people, and the girls who had no problem flirting with the opposite sex, I admired them. They were close to me. My twin was a social butterfly, and my best friend was hands down, the most popular girl in school. However, I just knew that I wasn't that girl.

Feeling and being different and introverted can be a true challenge. It can make you not only question your intelligence but your beauty as well. Initially, I had a rough time not being as social as the people around me, but it was my mother who let me know it was ok to be myself. My mother gave the encouragement I needed to maintain my identity. I don't know what false representation of myself I would have turned into, had it not been for my mother. I would advise you to keep open communication with your parents. They might get on your nerves, but the irrefutable fact is that they love you, and only want the best for you.

They know who you are outside of school. They won't turn their backs on you, and you should take advantage of the experience and wisdom they already have. Parents are a very useful resource when it comes to the serious decisions you will need to make in high school and besides, who else will pay for your football game and prom tickets? Truth is, you need them.

In high school, because I didn't really know how the guys I liked felt about me, I didn't know how to act around them. Additionally, I really, really, really, hated the idea of rejection. I still do. Anyway, to make a long story short, it was a mess. I had no problem communicating with males in general, but when it came to the few (and I mean few) guys I liked, that was another story.

Please don't be ashamed if you're still a little freaked out when it comes to dating guys, or even speaking with the one you might like. One thing you will discover in life is that the whole crush thing never gets old. Those butterflies, and the need to endlessly discuss everything concerning the guy you like, will never get old. It's completely normal at any age to repeatedly discuss that one time your crush did that thing that was so normal, yet so amazing because he did it. Crushes are simply a rite of passage through life. Yet, we know the goal is to establish a relationship one day, right? Right.

It is very true that some people begin dating, kissing, sex, etc., all before high school even starts. However, we also know that those experiences aren't the "real" experiences that we consider once we reach high school. When one reaches high school, one can no longer reflect on the flings of middle school, and God forbid discussing something that happened before then. So, here we are, the beginning of your recorded love life, high school.

High school is the place where we as young ladies are now somewhat (if not very much so) intrigued by guys. And we're most likely looking at the oh-so-beautiful senior athletes. If not them, then definitely the fresh faces in homeroom that make your unspeakable middle school crush look like a child. My advice, in terms of guys, is simple. I would simply tell you to take cautious risks. Calculate the pros and cons of a situation, prepare yourself for any possible result you can think of, and if it's worth it to you, go for it. Have fun. Take chances, but be wise in your decision making at the same time. Speak to him first, ask him out on a date maybe, but make sure you're mentally and emotionally prepared for whatever happens next.

On the side of caution, I would ask you to be very careful with guys. They can easily become everything you think about. Even when you're on track, they'll just pop up in your head. It's crazy. However, on the side of risk, I would ask that you take a few chances. You never know, your high school sweetheart might be one risk away. I'm not advising you to just go do stupid things because you think you can handle the consequences. Just don't be too cautious to the point that you don't enjoy your time in high school.

Overall, try your hardest not to wrap your life around guys. And if you happen to go through a breakup in high school, just know that college and better-looking men are just a few years away. You know you're going to college, right? Right.

Ah, yes that mandatory element of education, teachers. Can't deal with them, can't graduate without them. It's a love-hate relationship. Personally, I got along with the meanest teachers. I don't know what that says about me, but whatever. All jokes aside, most of the teachers you meet you will only tolerate. The only reason you would step foot into their classroom is because if you didn't, you'd get suspended. You don't want those problems, so you go to class. Simple. Not that they're horrible people, you just don't relate to them.

Like parents, these beings can provide you with some form of guidance, a great benefit when it comes to high school survival. They even go into the realm of college, when they help you by providing you with letters of recommendation. Always keep that in mind. I didn't, but I was a pretty awesome student. I didn't have to struggle to get letters written and I don't want you to get blindsided by required letters of recommendation when it is time to fill out your college or scholarship applications.

As stated earlier, you will only tolerate most of your teachers. However, there should always be a level of respect between you and the teacher. Additionally, outside of the teachers you tolerate, there will be a few that you really can't stand, and a few that you really can't make it without.

My advice concerning teachers would be to appreciate them. Even the ones you don't like. It really isn't until after graduation that you appreciate what they do for you. I really can't explain it, but a few teachers end up feeling like family. It's like they become school moms who keep you in line and help you elevate to the next phase in life. A few teachers start off as just teachers but end up becoming personal counselors, confidants, mentors, and devoted friends. You never know which teacher will become that advisor and confidant for you. It happens very unexpectedly. But when you find her/him, their impact on your life will forever change you.

When I first met my school mom, I didn't know what to think of her. She had just replaced one of my favorite instructors, and I felt a little offended when I saw her. I remember asking her, as she sat at her desk, "Who are you?" She said, "Mrs. Daniel, who are you?" It was weird because I didn't expect to hear so much confidence in her response. I remember telling her my name, and I think we spoke for about 10 more seconds, and the conversation was over. I never really expected to take any of her classes, let alone like her. But meeting her was one of the best things that ever happened to me in high school. Without her, I would have never taken two Virtual Enterprise courses, which exposed me to business and e-commerce and allowed me to find my true passion for entrepreneurship. It's very funny how life works out, especially in high school. You think you've lost your favorite teacher, only to gain a lifetime friend and an influence that will always have a place in your heart. Also note, I'm not saying this just because this is for her book. She knows how I feel about her outside of any written document.

Regardless of anything else, keep your academics first. You might hate a class. You might think it's stupid. You may know for a fact that the teacher is unworthy of his/her title. However, your GPA is one of the single most influential factors in high school. That silly drama class requires just as much effort as that history class. Get the grades first, and life will be much easier later. Some people, myself included, don't do to well on standardized tests. However, God, good recommendations, and my GPA allowed me to get into a university that had a 35% acceptance rate at the time of my admittance. Keep the grades up.

During high school, if you're anything like me, you will start to experiment with and discover the things that will shed light on who you truly are. I'm not saying that through these things you will reveal yourself completely, but most likely you'll look back and see that something in high school created the spark for you to pursue your career or dream. My advice to you would be to explore all your options and do it early. Sports will keep you in shape, and clubs will sharpen your mind. It's a win-win situation.

Extra-curricular activities shape you into a "well-rounded" student. Colleges look for students who are involved. Join a club, and become the president. Get on a team, and win awards. Colleges really eat that stuff up. Outside of the benefits towards college, extra-curricular activities allow you to be social. One of the hardest things to do is be social in a new setting. Having a team or group of associates behind you makes it a lot easier. It's one more element that can bring excitement and purpose into your high school career.

If I could go back, the only thing I would change is not joining a sports team. It's the only thing I did not do. Overall, my best survival tip is to keep your priorities straight. You can have all the fun you want after you take care of your studies.

Chapter 1: Who Am I?

One thing is for sure, if you enter high school as a person without standards and boundaries set, your many roller coaster experiences will define who you are and unfortunately, not in an enjoyable way. High school is a place where you are immediately thrust into classes, organizations, and activities with students who will be in college the following year. A few months ago, you were sitting with students your age and now you're sitting next to someone who will be leaving to take on the real world in the very near future. These people will undoubtedly become huge influences in your life without them even trying. You will be exposed to new mindsets, cultures, and beliefs relatively fast. Behaviors you have only seen on TV or in movies will be up close and personal for your viewing pleasure. It is imperative for you to know who you are and what you stand for before entering high school.

Many students enter their high school doors with no plan. They are just happy to be in high school. They have no plan for their future, but they are happy because there are only four more years before they are out on their own and that's all they are concerned with. They will be grown! YES! While this is true, these same students tend to experience quite a few challenges and stumbling blocks that could have been prevented if there was a plan in place. What is your ultimate goal? What do you plan to gain from high school? Why are you here? What are your likes and dislikes? What rules have you set in place? Have you clearly defined your boundaries? For example, if you don't like drinking or drugs, what will be your response when you are offered a drink or some pills? These situations and others happen more often than you think. So how will you handle them? Honestly, the best course of action is to already have a response to situations that are not in line with your goals. This exit strategy will allow you to effectively navigate past the distractions.

It may sound farfetched and you *could* possibly make it through high school and never be approached with the opportunity to try drugs or alcohol, have sex, or skip school. It's highly unlikely, but hey, it could happen. Why take that chance? Sit down and take time to determine who you are, where you want to go in life, and what your boundaries are. It's a relatively effortless process to do. Just scroll through your social media timeline and make a list of activities you see teenagers doing. Take that list and outline the activities you would like to be associated with and the ones you don't want to be associated with. Then, set your boundaries. Your will's and your will not's. This is a crucial step in navigating through high school successfully. Failing to plan for these potential obstacles pretty much guarantees you won't be prepared to escape the peer pressure that will come your way, and this lack of preparation will result in many of those "had to learn the hard way" situations.

←——————————————————————→

Dee Jay, 23, College Student, Major - Health Sciences

Having my parents around during my high school experience was such a blessing. Although my biological father wasn't around, my step dad stepped up and played a major part in my life. It was an amazing feeling when they would come support me since I was heavily involved with sports. I was in a relationship all through high school with the same person. I don't regret it because we are still together and we're blessed with a baby boy. If I could go back, I would've focused more on my future endeavors, like the best college for me, my career path, and learning the importance of my credit score.

While in school, I didn't bond with many of my teachers. I found out later that this is essential to getting into college, receiving internships, etc. because when the times comes, you will need reliable references to speak on your behalf. Also, being involved in positive activities while in high school is the best experience a teen can imagine. It gives you the chance to make friends, bond with people you wouldn't think about speaking with. Not only is it socially important, but you can get full scholarships for involvement in sports and clubs. Being involved in sports or clubs and having encounters with different people can put you in the right position for opportunities after high school.

I wouldn't want my high school experience to be any different because it taught me so much. Falling out with "close friends", the ugly looks, and being talked about prepared me for what life would be like in the adult world.

My advice to you is to complete your four years successfully, do what makes you happy, and enjoy high school the best way possible. Yeah, everybody won't like you but that's not why you are there. Focus on what career path you want to study in college, network early, and make relationships with your teachers that will last forever because that's one thing that I do regret not doing. Go to prom, all the games, and take pleasure in being a teenager while you are still able.

$$\longleftarrow\longrightarrow$$

Chapter 2: Every Adult Is Not Against You

Contrary to widespread belief we, the adults, are not the enemy. I know it may seem like we are, but we are NOT! In fact, we are your biggest supporters. You probably won't be able to understand this until much later in life but trust me, it's true. As a teacher and coach, I see so many girls put their trust in their peers. Do you really think that's a clever idea? The peers you are choosing to trust for guidance have basically had the same experiences as you. All they can do is share what they would do if they were in your shoes; but, where are they getting their information from? Have they *even* tried the advice they are giving you for themselves? And if so, how did it work for them? You should have the answers to these questions before you accept the advice of your peers.

The adults in your life, your parents, and teachers probably have great advice for many of the questions or problems that you have. However, for fear of hearing something contrary to what you want to do, you probably won't ask them. Isn't it ironic how ultimately you end up coming to us adults for advice on how to get yourself out of the situation anyway? Life would be much simpler if you just found the courage to talk to us beforehand. I think it's important for you to know that we will not always agree; however, we will always have your best interest at heart.

No matter how much you think you know, you don't know it all and I'm willing to bet that some of what you think you know is incorrect. How can you know how to handle situations you've never experienced? High school is a period of growth and outcomes are always better when you have experienced people guiding you. Trial and error proves valuable from time to time, but it should not be the norm. It may not seem like it now, but your parents will become your best friends when it's time for that transition to occur. Be patient and wait because that time isn't now. You need the guidance and advice of your parents and teachers more than you will ever know.

Once you get to the point where your mind begins to shift from teenager to young adult, you will begin to see that the adults in your life were looking out for your future, not your present. Many people today will tell you how thankful they are for a "no" they received many years ago. Some of those no's saved lives while others prevented terrible mistakes from occurring. Learn to trust the adults in your life. Don't rush the process, trust the process.

You may feel as though you don't have a relationship with your parent that is built on mutual trust. I have taught girls who have come from homes where they could not confide in the adults in their household. If that is you, find a good mentor. Open up and talk with a teacher or your guidance counselor. They will be able to help you find a mentor who will help guide you throughout your high school years. Many mentor/mentee relationships last well beyond high school. Girls tend to experience more life altering situations than boys and it is important to have someone capable of providing sound guidance and advice in your life. There is power in linking up with people who will hold you accountable.

←——————————————————→

Lorielle Flentall, 24, Future Registered Nurse

Looking back on my life, I'm finally realizing how important my time in high school was. At the time, I was only focused on having a good time. In my household, our mom was very strict when it came to academics. I would get good grades just so I could hang out with my friends. I was taking honors classes and most of the work was very easy to me. I rarely studied but never failed an assignment or test. Had I applied myself and focused on what came after graduating high school, I would be a lot further along in life than where I am today. High school is not the end of the road. The end of your high school years is honestly the beginning of the next level of your life. What you decide to do in the years following high school will determine where you will be and how hard you will have to work in the future.

Take advantage of every opportunity given to you. Don't get so lost in a boy or in what's going on around you.

Your parents may seem as if they don't want you to enjoy your life or even have one, but in all honestly, they do. I was blessed with a great mother and now, six years after graduating high school, I can say every problem I've had in life since graduating could have been avoided had I listened to my mama. She was literally right about everything. I am a 24-year-old mother of two boys and I have to work three times harder than my friends just to maintain. Had I listened to my mama and took advantage of every opportunity given to me, I wouldn't be in this situation. High school may not seem like a big deal to you now but trust me, how you proceed through these next few years can and will determine the course of your future.
Be prepared, Be patient, and Be smart.

Chapter 3: Decision Making

Let's face facts. From now on, the decisions you make will have a tremendous outcome on your future. Coming into high school, you will initially feel like you have all the time in the world to get things in order; but before you know it, senior year will have arrived. The decisions you made along the way will determine whether your senior year is full of excitement and expectations or worry and frustrations.

Making the conscious decision to place academics before your social life is key. I know it seems like it will make high school boring but it does just the opposite. Getting good grades and being a student with leadership qualities opens many doors of opportunity. Teachers will recommend you for opportunities to represent the school. Community leaders will begin to recognize you for your diligence and determination and you will begin to develop good habits that will transfer beyond high school into the real world. None of this may seem important right now, but your future self will be happy because your present self chose to make decisions that created a path to success.

Mindset is the key word. Eric Thomas said, "take advantage of the opportunity of a lifetime during the lifetime of the opportunity." You've got one shot at high school. That's it. It's up to you to make it the best possible experience. You must outline your priorities and make conscious decisions to focus on those priorities first and distractions last. It's tough, but it's necessary. Peer pressure is real. That's why your plan is so important. Yes, that cute boy will be at the party, but you have a test tomorrow. What's more important the boy or your goals? If he means that much to you, he should understand that your grades come first and he should be pushing you to study; but, we will discuss situations like this more in the relationship chapter.

Stop making permanent decisions with a temporary mindset. The choices you make in the present will impact the future. While experience is the best teacher, sometimes the lessons learned are not always easy to process or move on from. Ten years from now you will probably wish you would have "played the tape to the end" instead of going with the "Just Do It" philosophy. The methods are the same for achieving your goals. It all starts with your decision-making capabilities. If you want better grades, set standards, eliminate the distractions, and prioritize differently. If you want to improve your behavior, set standards, eliminate the distractions, and act and react differently. If you want better friends, set standards, eliminate the distractions, and choose peers wisely. THE PROCESS IS THE SAME. Your present self will make your future self very happy if you commit to making the right choices now.

While we are talking about making good decisions, let's talk about social media. OMG!! I don't know which causes more fights amongst girls in high school, boys or social media. Not only is social media full of negativity but it is a huge time waster. While there may be some boys in my classes that I have to remind a few times to put their phones away, I am consistently reminding many of the girls. It is as if they are defining who they are by how many likes they receive on the pictures they post. It's more important for *you* to look in the mirror and not only like who you see but love who you see.

Stop wasting your time trying to be accepted and focus on being your best you. When you love everything about you, flaws and all, the people who accept you for who you are will automatically navigate towards you. In high school, I see many girls change how they talk, how they dress, and how they act just to fit in with the people who seem to be "cool." They are trying to impress people who in all actuality, probably won't even be around in a year or two. I see girls giving shout outs to their "BFFs" and "Day

1s" on Monday only to be barely speaking to one another by Thursday. Spend more time focusing on the impression your teachers and counselors have of you because they are the ones who will be asked to write the letters of recommendations you will need for college and scholarship applications. I've worked as a college Director of Financial Aid and not once did I ever ask a prospective student to send me a letter of reference from their "BFF" or their "Day 1". Focus on what you will need in the future, not what you think you need right now.

Social media is a valuable tool when used properly. Find positive people to follow on social media. There are some very influential people who dedicate their lives to inspiring others to be the best they can be. You are not forced to follow the drama, you are *deciding* to follow the drama. **Never underestimate the power of words. Exposure to negativity will breed negative thoughts that often come out in the form of low self-esteem, depression, foul language, hateful attitudes, etc.** The power of the delete button is underrated. When someone sends you something negative, simply delete it instead of responding. That removes the power and control from the person who is trying to bait you into a negative situation. Your decision to delete the person puts you in the driver's seat.

You would think social media is the modern day young girls' diary. This is another reason why you should keep a journal. If you are going through something, write about the situation in your journal, NOT in a public forum for the world to see because once it's there, it's there. Most incidents in school wouldn't even happen if social media was nonexistent. For the life of me, I can't understand how people who live in the same neighborhood and see each other multiple times before coming to school decide to wait until they are at school to have an argument or fight. The only reason I can think of is that they have an audience at school. Pouring out your issues into your journal and finding positive ways to solve them won't lead to ISS or OSS like an altercation will.

Be careful what you post on social media. Always remember, the delete button only deletes it from *your* view. It is still accessible. Can you imagine being called to the front office and seeing your parents there when you arrive? You have no clue what's about to happen until your parents start asking you about certain comments you made via social media/text. But wait a minute, you deleted all of that. How did they find out? Surprise! It hasn't been deleted from some other places. Certain people have the authority to retrieve deleted messages/posts. I have had a school resource officer describe the scene of a parent who was presented with the full transcript of a conversation and not just the version their daughter showed them. It wasn't a pretty scene.

Time plays a major factor in decision making. Giving yourself time to calm down and come off the emotional roller coaster you are riding will allow you to look at the situation differently. I cannot tell you the number of times I have spoken with students after an argument or altercation and they always think differently about the situation because they are in a different mindset. The punishment has been handed down and they are no longer thinking about it from their raging emotions' point of view. Unfortunately, now they see it from the "look what I've gotten myself into" point of view.

Speaking of those "look what I've gotten myself into" moments, these tend to happen when I talk with some girls after they have moved forward with their decision to lose their virginity to a guy they thought they loved, only to have him not pay them any attention the next day. Like I said previously, the adults are the ones you turn to *after* the fact instead of before because you really don't want to be steered away from the choice you want to make. You want to go with your decision. Now, the chase is over and you're having trouble understanding why he is not answering your texts or phone calls. Here's why--there were two different mindsets approaching the same situation. In most cases, one (the boy) was focused on getting what he wanted and the other (the girl) was focused on getting what she thought she needed. One got what they wanted but the other person didn't receive what they thought they needed. Now, you're left with feelings of betrayal, hurt, abandonment, embarrassment, etc. Feelings you did not experience before you made the decision to move forward.

When a young impressionable girl goes through this type of experience, she tends to spiral out of control. The adults in her life notice the change in behavior. It seems like that girl who once was a sweet, innocent, trusting young girl in love turns into a completely different person. She begins to put on masks to cover the pain and hurt. She is determined to never go through this painful situation again. In her mind, she *knows* how to handle guys like him now. That is until the next guy shows her the attention she is seeking and there she goes again with the same cycle. That cycle will not end until she addresses the root causes - low self-esteem, a lack of self-awareness, and failure to create a plan for success with a reasonable set of boundaries and rules incorporated. Don't be that girl.

Figure out who you are and where you want to go in life then develop your plan of action.

←————————————————————————→

Teantra Blackwell, 24, Future Registered Nurse

One of the most important things to remember while going through high school is to ALWAYS REMAIN FOCUSED. I say that because you can have goals or your mind set on something that you want to do but it is so easy to get distracted.

I would like to spend a minute, or two, maybe five (lol) on a topic I feel like most young girl's face. That would be BOYS of course. There are some nice, handsome, and talented guys out here. Most girls want to be known as the girl that is dating a popular guy.

Truth is, in high school, you don't realize how big the world is and how many opportunities you can have if you remain focused. I was one of the girls that lost focus while I was in high school. I had goals I wanted to accomplish in life but like I said, I lost focus. I was on the varsity basketball team and everything was PERFECT until "mother nature" decided not to visit me one month. On my seventeenth birthday, I found out I was pregnant. When I found out, it felt like my heart dropped to the floor. I was scared. I didn't know how to tell my parents, my coaches, or the guy.

I won't go into many details but let's just say my pregnancy was awful. During my senior year, I was barely eighteen with a newborn baby trying to maintain good grades while being a young mother and playing basketball. It was harder than I ever imagined but my parents helped a lot. I didn't have a job so how could I possibly take care of a child. I don't want to imagine what it would be like if my parents were not around to help me. I managed to graduate high school and then I went to college for a semester but dropped out. I tried college again later and dropped out again. Ladies, I just want you all to stay focused and hold on to your dreams tightly. I'm still holding onto my goal to become a registered nurse but it is taking me longer than others because I have responsibilities I have to take care of now.

It is best to keep yourself involved in some type of extra-curricular activities. I'm not saying you shouldn't have a boyfriend but you need to be smart and think about your future always. There will be more handsome, nice, and talented guys after your high school years, so don't jeopardize your future. I love my babies and will do anything under the sky for them, but I also know my life would have been completely different than it is now had I been more focused. My life isn't bad but it's not great either and having children at an early age won't stop me from achieving my dreams. My best advice to you would be - THINK of your future and REMAIN FOCUSED.

Chapter 4: Relationships

This undoubtedly will be a complex chapter because it covers more than what immediately comes to mind, a romantic type relationship. This chapter covers relationships with people in general and why it is important to choose your circle of influence wisely. An old proverb says, "Tell me who your friends are and I will tell you who you are." Another version of the proverb says, "Show me your friends and I'll show you your future." The people you choose to associate with says a great deal about you as a person and your goals and aspirations in life. People with a clear plan do not choose to hang with people who have no plan. It presents a conflict of interest. Their mindsets are not in agreement.

When you link up with people who are like-minded and are progressing in the same direction, your journey becomes easier. You share common interests and you offer support for each other. You are not in a constant discussion about why you can't do something that they are eager to do. Never underestimate the power of spring cleaning! That same process you use to get rid of clothes, shoes, and other items you no longer need should be applied to your life as well. Get rid of the people, things, and habits that keep drawing you back to disappointment and hurt. They should be bagged up and discarded just like those pants you wore back in sixth grade. They were cute and everybody commented with #slay on your picture when you posted it on social media, but they don't fit anymore.

When you begin to grow, you will see that some people just don't grow with you. High school is a time where you will be exposed to new ideas and insights. Some of them you will like, some of them you won't. Some of your friends from middle school will not have the same interests that you do. It's okay. Some people will go their separate ways and that's not always a terrible outcome. Sometimes your Day 1s need to be repositioned and recategorized. It's hard to grow when you are around the people you've always been around. Who challenges who to be better in this type of relationship? It doesn't mean there is something wrong with you or them, it just means you're growing in different directions. The key is to recognize the growth and embrace it because when you do, you will find that people who share your new mindset will appear and you will build new relationships. Be choosy when it comes to your circle of friends. Understand the difference between friends and acquaintances and place people in the right category. And remember, to have a friend you must be a friend.

Now onto the relationship topic that contributes to so much anxiety for teen girls. Dating! Whew. Here we go. Dating in high school is interesting, to say the least. I've seen it all. I've had girls crying in my classroom during the relationship and after the relationship ended. I continuously see girls fighting over guys. Strange thing though, I don't see many boys fighting over girls these days. Why do you think that is? Maybe because there are so many who make themselves easily accessible. Girls are not exclusive and rare finds anymore. It almost seems as though they have placed themselves on the sale rack and discounted their value as affordable for anyone. Why would he stress the loss of a girl when there are 10-15 other ones in his DM and inbox each day? Why are two girls in a fight over this boy who is obviously playing them both? Why does the boy always get off Scot-free? Why are there two girls' names on the OSS list who are missing valuable instruction time because they are suspended, but the boy is in school walking past my classroom with his arm around a new girl? What's really going on here? There is a significant shift that needs to take place in the minds of teen girls. This mind shift needs to occur before the madness begins, not after the unpleasant experience.

A great deal of the madness and drama girls tend to be involved in stems from getting involved in situations that require more emotional and mental stability than they have at the current moment. They end up in situations that are beyond their level of experience so they make decisions with no prior knowledge or understanding to base their decisions upon. Before entering high school, you must be prepared to balance all of these new experiences appropriately.

Your level of self-awareness and self-esteem will play an important part in establishing healthy relationships. I've had many discussions with teen girls regarding why they choose to wear certain clothes to school. The main reason I hear is "because I think it's cute." It may be cute for the beach, but not for school. If they were honest with themselves and me, they would probably say, "I wore this so he would notice me." Unfortunately, they rarely think about everyone else that notices them. In some instances, I have seen girls get extremely upset because of the comments said to them by a boy they were not interested in dating. What did you expect? There is no secret button you can push that only allows you to be seen by the boy you are interested in dating. The entire student body and staff see you. You wanted to get a smile from one boy but you end up getting unwanted advances from others as well. Some things should be left to the imagination and not easily accessible. If this pattern of behavior continues, you will begin to see that the guys you are dating are not interested in you, they are interested in what you have been showing them. This tends to lead to those situations we discussed earlier. It wasn't a relationship that he was after. For a guy to respect you, he must first see that you respect yourself.

Some boys are just not ready to settle down and nothing you do will change that. Like you, they must go through their own journey to become who they are destined to be. Make sure you do not become a casualty of the war they are fighting. This tends to happen to the freshmen girls more than any other. For some reason, they tend to believe that because the senior boys are paying them lots of attention, they must be the "baddest" girl on campus. Sorry, but no, that is not why the senior boy is after you. Trust me on this. One of my teacher friends shared her personal story about this very situation. She said, "my first boyfriend was a senior my freshman year and I thought it was the best thing that ever happened! He began to pressure me to do stuff physically, but I held back. After about a month he broke up with me. I, of course, was devastated! A month later, he had gotten another girl pregnant and I realized how much of a bullet I had dodged!" Now for me, I too had a brief relationship with a senior boy when I was a freshman in high school. He was cute and he was an athlete so I thought I was #winning! We didn't really go on real dates because I was a freshman and couldn't really go anywhere. We hung out in school and we would meet up at games or school functions. On certain nights, I would arrive at the game late, because I had to find transportation. When I would get there, I would see him sitting with a girl and he really wouldn't acknowledge me. I would ask who the girl was and he would say, "my cousin." Now the first couple of times, I didn't really question his response. However, one night at a basketball game, it happened again. After walking away, I saw his brother and I asked him if the girl was their cousin and he said, "no." At that moment, I figured the other girls weren't either and he had probably been lying to me the entire time. His cover was blown so he broke up with me. I was #devastated just like my friend.

$\longleftarrow\hspace{3cm}\longrightarrow$

Keondra Flentall, 24, Drawing Operator

High School was an interesting experience for me and interesting is the only word I could come up with at the moment to describe those years.

On April 2, 2001, my dad died and my life was never the same again. I was eight years old when I lost my father and my life changed forever after that. My dad was my best friend. Growing up without him is something I've never really learned to accept but, I've come to live with the loss. I was forced to grow up fatherless and I had no say so in the matter. Despite losing my father, I had a phenomenal mother who raised five kids on her own! My mother taught us everything she could but in a way, it wasn't enough.

In 8th grade, I found what I thought was love and now looking back, I think that's probably what started this roller coaster called life for me. I was already dealing with other issues at home and to compound those issues, I was in an unhealthy relationship. I feel like if I hadn't lost my dad so young, I wouldn't have found myself falling in love with the first guy that gave me attention. For the next five years of my life, I spent my time chasing what I thought was the "perfect boyfriend" and in return. I got Mono, heartache, physically, mentally, and emotionally abused, and cheated on. Not your idea of a first love, huh?

High school was a nightmare for me. Even though I was a "popular" girl. I still had the hardest time coping with the day to day life of a teenage girl. Walking the halls of high school was satisfying yet traumatizing. I loved the feeling of having others look at me and go out of their way to speak to me. However, the low self-esteem I dealt with beneath the surface was really driving the need to have all the attention.

I thank God for the relationship I had with two of my teachers! Mrs. Dundore and Mr. Quintero believed in me when I thought about giving up. I thought about dropping out of school my senior year. I had already missed a third of the school year so why not drop out. If it wasn't for those two teachers, I wouldn't have graduated. It took two teachers looking beyond my behavior and seeing the potential in me for me to realize I was so much more than just a girl from a small town.

If I could go back and change anything about high school it would be my naivety. I was naive to the fact that high school is more than proms, pep rallies, football games and graduation night. High school should've been my time to find myself instead of trying to be the person everyone wanted me to be. I graduated in 2010 and sometimes I wake up in disbelief. How could so much of my life have flown by so fast? Stay focused and make good decisions not matter what obstacle you face.

If you dream big, you receive big! The world is your footstool. Being a woman is a blessing and you have the power to move mountains. Boys will always be around. Focus on being the best version of yourself. Always be you because the right person will "feel" the real you. Excel in high school! Go to college! Travel the world! Spread your wings! This is your time!

←————————————————————→

Give yourself the time you need to experience life a little more before you try and take the committed relationship step. You will find yourself having fewer regrets later in life. It's difficult to find someone with the same mindset and goals when you yourself don't have a plan or any goals. But to be honest, you really shouldn't be worrying about finding someone anyway. Your focus should be on yourself and your education. Whatever you do though, do not settle for the sake of being able to say,

48

"that's BAE." There are a couple of signs to watch for that would indicate that he *shouldn't* be BAE anyway.

- You're studying formulas and equations for your next exam, but he's studying the cheat codes so he can reach the next level on his video game.
- You're studying the parts of the body for your biology test, but he's studying the parts of the body of the girl who is available at the time.

High school is not speed dating. Don't get caught up in the hype. If the boy doesn't respect himself, he won't respect you and he will ultimately pull you down before you lift him up. SLOW DOWN. Take it all in stride and use your experiences as preparation for the next level. It will seem like this process is dragging on forever and everyone has a boyfriend but you. Trust me when I say that is not the case. The only reason it seems that way is because you have placed having a BAE at the top of your priority list. There will be plenty of great guys around when you are ready and the timing is right. Don't get caught up in the peer pressure and end up settling for the ones that walk up with their pants halfway to their knees saying, "What's up Shawty?" Don't be so anxious to find someone before you find yourself. You will enjoy the experience more if you take the time to do it right. Wise up and envision yourself with a king. Establish and follow your plan so you don't get caught wasting time with the king's jester.

49

I'm not saying that all boys are bad, as a matter of fact, I'm not saying that any of them are. All I am saying is that it will take time and patience to sift through to the ones who really have their goals and plans together and will join you on your journey to becoming your best you because they understand the importance of their journey to becoming their best as well. Here is a little tip. Talk to a teacher you trust about the boy you're interested in dating. Teachers see them from a different viewpoint and can offer valuable insight because you're probably only looking at his physical appearance. We grade their assignments!! We know how their minds work! LOL!

◄────────────────────────────────►

Cortni, 25, Pharmacist

I'll start by giving a little background about myself so that you understand where I come from. I was raised in a little community in South Carolina. Growing up, and still, I didn't have a good relationship with my mama. Although we never went without food, or shelter, or other necessities, we were poor. My mama made a minimum wage salary. I knew that we were not well off, so I very rarely asked her for any money or to pay for anything. Once I was old enough to work, I paid for everything myself. Including my car, my gas, my clothes, my vacations, and my cheerleading expenses. My biological father was not involved in my life. I went to visit him every other weekend up until I turned six or seven. After that, I only saw him a few times.

When I was in high school, I ran cross-country, track, and cheered. I only remember my mama coming to one cross-country meet, no track meets, and a handful of football games. I was always jealous of my friends because their parents were still married; actively involved in everything they did, and attended all awards and sporting events they had. Now that I have children of my own, I am thankful that I was forced to understand what it felt like to not know if your parents loved you. I believe it has made me a better mama. But, as a teenager it made me look for love in other ways.

I started dating a boy named Justin almost as soon as I started high school. I wanted every single minute of his time. I wanted him to only want to spend time with me. I wanted him to give up everything else he liked so he could be with me. We dated all through high school. When he went off to college during my senior year, I didn't feel that love anymore. So, as soon as another boy was there to make me feel loved, I ran with it. Unfortunately, boy number two was just recently released from jail when we started dating. He used drugs and slept with many, many girls. But, when you're seventeen, and he makes you feel the love you've been looking for, you don't believe anything that anybody else tells you about him. He ended up being sent back to jail about a month after we got together. I got into a fight with my mama over him, got arrested, and wasn't allowed to go back to live with her. I moved in with his grandmother and visited him religiously in jail. I missed many days of school for his court dates. I didn't keep up with my homework and tests the way that I normally would. Luckily my GPA was high enough that even having a semester of less than par performance, I still graduated valedictorian. After about seven months of not talking to my family, I rode by my mama's house and Justin was there. That day saved my life. We are now married, with two kids.

If I could give you any advice on boys, it would be to not become obsessed with them. Do not look for missing parts of your life in them. Work hard to love yourself before you try to love anyone else or use the love of a boy to feel complete. I've been out of high school for eight years and I'm just now learning the importance of loving myself. If you can love yourself, things people say about you will not bother or influence you as much.

During my last semester of high school, there was one teacher that consistently tried to talk sense into me without condemning my choices. She was the one person I knew that I could talk to and she would be brutally honest in a way that didn't feel extremely judgmental. If you're lucky enough to have a teacher in your school that cares about you and tells you the truth when nobody else will; listen to them. The truth is difficult to hear when you think that you've got it all figured out but, it may keep you from going down the completely wrong path. Look for a mentor in high school; somebody that will listen and offer honest, selfless advice. Remember that the teachers who you think "just don't understand," have already walked in your shoes. They know what you're dealing with and they just want you to avoid learning the hard way like they did. If your parents are not actively involved in your life, accept when someone else is willing to step in and love you. I was lucky enough to have a pharmacist come into my life and give me direction; although, I didn't appreciate it as much as I should have at the time.

Academics in high school are more important than they've been during the other years of your school career. Colleges do not care what kind of obstacles you have overcome to just barely graduate. They do not care if your mother or father were not involved. They care about your GPA, your test scores, and any extra-curricular activities you were involved in. I was accepted to every college I applied to because of my GPA. I had a choice in the college

I attended. I had enough scholarship money to pay for my schooling, housing, meal plan, books, and I had extra money left over to spend. Don't ever let something distract you from your academics. One thing that can never be taken away from you is your education. Education is the key to success. You don't have to be at the top of your class to do well in college. In fact, I've seen several people who were very bright in high school get so distracted by the social scene of college that they flunk out of a university and must finish later at a local college. It's great to have fun, but don't let it knock you off your game. Stay focused and driven and it will pay off.

I mentioned involvement in extra-curricular activities is important for college but, it's important during high school as well. There will be so many opportunities for you to get involved in the hustle and bustle outside of school. (drugs, alcohol, and partying) If you are held accountable by a coach, or leader, you're less likely to give into that peer pressure. If you find something that you love to do, get involved. It will keep you from having time to do things that can potentially set you way back. If you've grown up in a household of drugs and alcohol, let that be the reason you stay away from them. I never drank a single alcoholic drink in high school because I had already witnessed the destruction it can cause.

If I could go back and change one thing in high school, it would be the day I broke up with Justin. That day changed the rest of my high school career and could have prevented me from being valedictorian, going to college, or graduate school.

The best advice I can give you to make it through high school successfully is to not get caught up in what is considered cool at the time. Cool things change every day but a high school diploma and a college degree will stay with you forever.

$\longleftarrow\!\!\!\longrightarrow$

Chapter 5: Enjoy Your High School Years

"We are what we repeatedly do. Excellence then is not an act, but a habit." Aristotle

Your level of success in high school depends greatly upon the habits you establish early in your high school career. Establishing good habits will help you navigate through high school effectively. Now more than ever, there are students who are graduating in three years instead of four. Students are enrolling in college through dual enrollment programs and they are working on their high school diploma and a college degree at the same time. Only people with an effective plan and good habits can create these types of opportunities. When you set goals for your future a set of boundaries should automatically become attached. There will be places you can no longer go, people you can no longer hang around, and activities you can no longer do. Understand that distractions will come. You must be focused and have the right mindset so you can recognize the distractions and take the appropriate measures to stay focused.

Change your perspective about school. Figure out a way to unlearn any of the negative beliefs you currently have. High school is not a burden, it's a bridge. It's a part of your current journey that will get you from where you are to where you would like to go next. It would be very

54

difficult to get there without going through high school first. Having a positive mindset about school will help you see what it offers from a positive perspective. Think about it this way. If you hate liver and your mom texted you one morning and said she was preparing liver for dinner, your entire day would probably be consumed with negative thoughts about dinner. On the other hand, if you love liver, you would be excited. It's the same way with school. Get up every morning knowing that this is another opportunity to be the best student you can be instead of dreading going to school. There are so many opportunities for growth and you will not recognize them if you are not in the right mindset. Starting your day out thinking negatively will be the catalyst for a day filled with negativity.

It may not seem like it now but high school will be over before you know it and you need to be prepared to journey into the real world. The work you put in during these four years (or less) will undoubtedly determine the course of your next stage of life. Get involved, surround yourself with positive people and always remember that your future self can only live the life she wants to live if you put in the hard work now.

I cannot promise you that every day will be great but there are specific steps you can take to steer the course of each day in a positive direction. People who talk about changing rarely ever do, but people who take action begin to see changes taking place. Some events that happen may appear to be bad or unfair but after enough time passes, you will eventually see the reasoning and lesson behind the experience.

People will not be pleased with you all the time; that doesn't mean you should stop being pleasant. People will not like you all the time; that doesn't mean you should stop being likable. People will not tell you the truth all the time; that does not mean you should stop being truthful. In other words, who you are is not defined by the way you are treated, but by the way you treat others. Learn the lesson from the experience and move forward in life.

Take life one day at a time and embrace your journey. Settle yourself in and learn the ropes. Make new friends, join new clubs, go all out and run for a student body leadership position. Take time to weigh out the options before making life altering decisions based on emotions. Be patient and give the guy you will meet in college an opportunity to experience the best you and not the you with the broken heart and a ton of regrets from bad choices. Allow people to see the real you and not the person social media and reality TV encourages you to be.

It seems ideal to be able to say never judge a book by its cover but sometimes due to the appearance, language, and actions, it's impossible not to do so. Stop acting like you're auditioning for a role on the *Pretty Little Liars* show. Make your parents and yourself proud. You don't have to be the best there is; you just need be the best you can be. Refrain from comparing yourself to others and thinking they are better than you. They probably just tend to make better decisions than you.

Remember to keep a GROWTH MINDSET about everything. When I was in high school, I hated math. I felt like my math teachers used word problems just to drive me insane. I just couldn't understand why I needed to know when those two trains that left from different cities would meet. Math was never my favorite subject. I could get through the classes but it was a struggle. I can remember taking Statistics class in college. I cried through every test because I would stress myself out about math. For years I had a fixed mindset about the subject. I had always told myself I didn't like math and it was too hard so my mind's natural reaction was to immediately stress out when it was time to do math. Somehow, I earned good grades in both my college math courses. I didn't know then that the fear was all in my mind. I know now that the fear was caused by my fixed mindset. I hope you never develop a fixed mindset about anything. Just because it is hard, doesn't mean it's impossible. Learn how to overcome the challenges. They will make you stronger. Always be open to new possibilities. And since we are talking about math, I'm going to leave you with this math equation:

If X is my goal, how do I solve for X?

Establish your goals and the plan you need to accomplish them. Set your boundaries and follow your plan to success. Above all else, enjoy this new journey.

$$\longleftrightarrow$$

Lyric Johnson, 17, Fisk University Rising Freshman Full Academic and Athletic Scholarship

Parents are very important to your high school career, but then again, they aren't. You want a parent that lets you make the little mistakes that we all must learn from, but they should also be there to keep you from making dire mistakes. A supportive parent is awesome to a certain extent. Yes, you want mom to be there for you when you do well in school or athletically, but she shouldn't be there defending you when you're wrong. Not having a parental influence isn't necessarily bad for the child if they are strong willed and determined to be great. The child should use the resources around them to stay on track. So regardless if your parents are the best or the worst, high school is a time for you to learn and blossom into a young adult that can take care of yourself. If you don't have strong parental support, it's not the end of the world, if you're doing what you need to, and you're communicating with adults around you, you'll be fine!

Boys are the devil stay away! No, I'm kidding! High school is filled with boys and their hormones, even if they are a gentleman in front of you; they are still gross in their brain. They can't help it. You just have to make smart choices when choosing someone to affiliate with. Is he respectful to adults? Are his grades decent? Does he know what he wants to do when he gets older? He doesn't have to be perfect, but you do want someone who will treat you right and be a great friend before anything! I have a lot of friends who are "stuck in love", with terrible people. That reminds me... Please keep your body to yourself! People told me this on numerous occasions and you always think that it won't be you, but it doesn't take long. If you're going to lose your virginity, it's not the end of the world, but it isn't ideal. Just make sure you protect yourself and refrain from wasting it because it can only happen once, you don't want to regret that decision for the rest of your life.

Building relationships with your teachers is very important. They love to say that favorites don't exist, but I promise you this, any teacher you have a great relationship with will look out for you and your grade will be good. Teachers also give great insight because they have seen dozens of kids like you and they want you to do well. So, when you see a teacher showing you special attention, it's most likely because they see potential in you to be great! It took me a while to realize that, but as I got older I understood.

Everyone is going to tell you that academics are extremely important, unfortunately, they are right. The better your grades are, the more opportunities that will arise. It also makes you feel good. Grades are an example of how hard you work! You don't have to be "smart" to get good grades, you just have to do your work and ask for help when you need it. If you do that, good grades will come.

Participating in extracurricular activities is important because aside from grades, colleges want to know what separates you from everyone else. If you did great in school, and that's all, it doesn't make you seem diverse. So, put your hand in different cookie jars. Try different things, you never know what you will excel at!

If I could go back and change anything about high school, it would be a couple of things. One, I would have played other sports besides basketball. Don't get me wrong, ball is life, but my athletic abilities could have been enhanced. One other thing I would have changed is me being a pushover. I'm very nice, so a lot of people took advantage of me in my high school years. So instead of being bulldozed over, I would have stood my ground much more. Besides that, I enjoyed high school. You spend every day wishing to graduate, but once you do, you realize that it really wasn't that terrible. High school is literally what you make it.

I'm going to give you some behind the scenes advice rather than "do your work" or "stay focused." Yes, those are important, but everyone will tell you that. I will say for one, stay out of the drama, if "Rebecca" is talking about you, oh well, she is probably just jealous of how awesome you are. If someone likes the boy you like and wants to cause issues, oh well, it's not that serious. If you stay in drama, that's what you will be known for and you don't want that. Two, don't go to high school worried about your first relationship. School is for you to learn, not for you to be dating. When you are constantly looking for your next victim, you'll end up a single pringle; let it happen when it does, patience is key. Next, be yourself regardless of what anyone thinks about you, because it's not their life, it's yours! You must create your happiness in high school because there are low moments. The way you react and get yourself out of these moments is what's important. Don't let anyone's actions determine how you feel. Don't listen to rumors either; they are most likely made up because people love to talk. Most importantly, find yourself, you'll have more growing to do once you graduate, but you'll also grow a lot in high school. Let the process happen!

AN OPEN LETTER TO MY DAUGHTERS
Written by: Life

They said, "Life, you think you're better than somebody!"
I said, "Nah, I don't think I'm better than nobody; but, it
does bother me when people are bothered by me trying to
be better."
It's like somewhere in society we've decided it's alright to
be lesser; but it's a problem anytime you're trying to get
your life together. So, I'm like whatever, "Hi Haters, Hi
Haters!" I'm going to love you regardless it ain't for me to
harbor no hatred.
Knowing that I was created by the father of creation that's
why I don't have a problem looking into my daughter's
faces and telling them, you are destined for greatness!
Don't strive to MEET, strive to EXCEED expectations!
You ain't got to keep pace with nobody, GO HARDER!
Don't answer to every name that a man calls you!
And if a man says that you're beautiful tell him, "thank
you;" but know that you heard it first from your father so
you didn't need nobody to tell you!
In this life, there will be losses; but, as long as you learn
from your losses, you're not a failure!
Don't buy what the TV sells you; you're not made by the
clothes you put on! What makes you is loving and
respecting the cloth that you are cut from!
You're beautiful beyond measure from your complexion to
your hair texture!
Study to show yourself approved!
Choose to be an intellectual!
Articulate when you speak!
Don't denounce your education!
Over-stand the misunderstanding, there's no such thing
as talking Caucasian! Love what your race is, without
being a racist!
Hold your head up when you speak and look people
directly in their faces! Respect yourself and your elders!

Learn to stay away from drama!
Know that you can be somebody's wife before you're
somebody's baby momma!
Honor your mother and your father, even though you
know neither's perfect! You love them anyway and just
know that God is working!
You're not worthless, you have a purpose, I love you,
know what your worth is! You're more than a hairdo,
high heel pumps, and nice purses!
You give until it hurts! Then get down on your knees and
pray! Knowing that they talked about Jesus, you don't
worry about what these people say!
And the next time if they ask you, "Do you think you're
better than somebody?!"
You look them directly in their face! And say,
***"YES! I AM A BETTER ME TODAY THAN I WAS
YESTERDAY!"***
#VillageMinded-Life ~~ IG - @lifespeakslife

<u>Your Goals and Plans for Success Journal</u>

Journaling helps you grow in many ways. Use the following pages to journal your thoughts, questions, and experiences. Take time to establish clear goals, plans, and boundaries. Make sure you **WRITE THEM DOWN!** By doing so, you will have a written record of your progress. Below are some tips to help you solve that math equation I presented to you earlier.

<u>If X is my goal, how do I solve for X?</u>

- Take interest surveys and research careers
   a. Visit www.mynextmove.org
   b. Participate in job shadowing opportunities
- Research colleges
   a. Visit www.collegedata.com
- Set your goals
   a. Use the SMART Goal method
- Establish your boundaries
   a. Search your social media timelines for typical teen behavior. Decide what you will do and what you will not do.
- Establish a plan. Write it down.
   a. Do your best to stick to your plan but understand there will be speed bumps and detours. Have a plan to recover and get back on track to accomplishing your goals.
- Construct your vision board
   a. Fill your board with images that will remind you of your goals and your plan for success.
- Find a mentor to hold you accountable

<u>ENJOY YOUR JOURNEY!</u>

Kimberly Wilson Daniel

Kimberly Wilson Daniel

Kimberly Wilson Daniel

Kimberly Wilson Daniel

Kimberly Wilson Daniel

Kimberly Wilson Daniel

Kimberly Wilson Daniel

Kimberly Wilson Daniel

Kimberly Wilson Daniel

Kimberly Wilson Daniel

Kimberly Wilson Daniel

Kimberly Wilson Daniel

Kimberly Wilson Daniel

Kimberly Wilson Daniel

Kimberly Wilson Daniel

Kimberly Wilson Daniel

CPSIA information can be obtained
at www.ICGtesting.com
Printed in the USA
BVHW041147141218
535635BV00018B/238/P